Unlucky Randy

by Veronica Freeman Ellis
illustrations by Susan Avishai

Harcourt Brace & Company

Orlando Atlanta Austin Boston San Francisco Chicago Dallas New York Toronto London

"Go!" cried Randy. Randy, Ellie, and Mickey dashed across the field to the leafy tree.

Ellie ran more quickly than Mickey and Randy. "Chief and I win!" shrieked Ellie.

"You were just lucky," said Randy.

"Not lucky, Randy," replied Ellie. "Fast!"

Randy was grumpy. "Ellie, you were only lucky!" Randy said. "Bet you can't do it again!"

"Ready?" said Ellie.

"Get set," Randy said. "Go!" Randy, Ellie, and Mickey ran back.

Mickey passed Ellie, and then he passed Randy. This time Mickey shrieked, "Chief and I win!"

Now Randy was really grumpy. "You both were just lucky!" Randy said loudly.

"Good grief!" Mickey said. "Don't be so grumpy, Randy! It's only a race on a field."

"Yes, Mickey," Ellie agreed. "It's only a game. It's silly to be grumpy."

Randy turned slowly. "I'm sorry. I'm just sticky, dirty, AND thirsty."

Mickey and Ellie walked Randy home. Chief ran ahead. At Randy's house, Randy's sister Hayley was crying.

"Thief! Thief!" Hayley shrieked. "My bunny! Chief has Funny Bunny! Thief! Thief!"

"Chief!" yelled Randy. "Stop, Chief!"

"My bunny!" shrieked Hayley. "Chief will rip Funny Bunny to pieces!" Chief ran fast, but Randy ran faster.